LIGHTBOX

Go to
www.openlightbox.com
and enter this book's unique code.

ACCESS CODE

LBXB9997

Lightbox is an all-inclusive digital solution for the teaching and learning of curriculum topics in an original, groundbreaking way. Lightbox is based on National Curriculum Standards.

OPTIMIZED FOR
- ✓ TABLETS
- ✓ WHITEBOARDS
- ✓ COMPUTERS
- ✓ AND MUCH MORE!

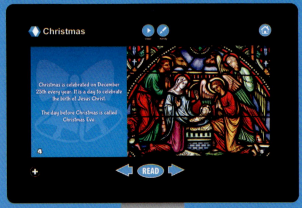

Copyright © 2021 Smartbook Media Inc. All rights reserved.

STANDARD FEATURES OF LIGHTBOX

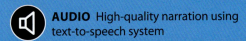
AUDIO High-quality narration using text-to-speech system

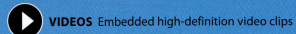
VIDEOS Embedded high-definition video clips

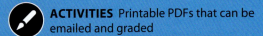
ACTIVITIES Printable PDFs that can be emailed and graded

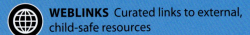
WEBLINKS Curated links to external, child-safe resources

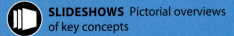
SLIDESHOWS Pictorial overviews of key concepts

INTERACTIVE MAPS Interactive maps and aerial satellite imagery

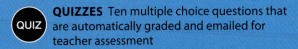
QUIZZES Ten multiple choice questions that are automatically graded and emailed for teacher assessment

KEY WORDS Matching key concepts to their definitions

VIDEOS

WEBLINKS

SLIDESHOWS

QUIZZES

New Year

CONTENTS

- 2 Lightbox Access Code
- 4 When Is New Year's Day?
- 6 What Is New Year's Day?
- 8 Janus
- 10 Where We Celebrate
- 12 Coming Together
- 14 How We Celebrate
- 16 More Traditions
- 18 Helping Others
- 20 Special Celebrations
- 22 New Year Facts
- 24 Key Words

New Year's Day is celebrated on January 1 every year. It is the first day of the new year.

Some cultures celebrate the New Year on a different date.

January 1 was first celebrated as **New Year's Day** in **46 BC**.

New Year's Day is celebrated by people all over the world. It is a time to celebrate the year that is about to begin.

Janus was a Roman god. His head had two faces. One face looked back at the old year. The other faced the new.

The month of January is named after him.

Thousands of people go to Times Square in New York City on December 31. A large ball drops down from the top of a building at midnight.

More than **1 billion** people watch the **Times Square ball** drop on television.

Fireworks light up the sky at midnight on January 1. People watch the fireworks with their family and friends.

There are special foods to eat on New Year's Day. In the United States, many people eat black-eyed peas, cabbage, and ham.

These foods are thought to bring good luck.

People enjoy going to parades on New Year's Day. Some also watch a football game.

The biggest New Year's parade in the United States is in Pasadena, California. It is called the Rose Parade.

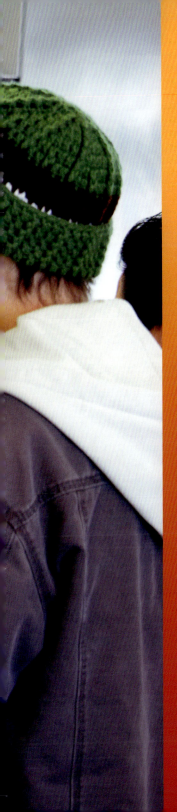

Many people make New Year's resolutions. Resolutions are like promises.

Some people choose to help others more. They might donate money to a charity or volunteer in their community.

At midnight, people sing "Auld Lang Syne." Everyone stands in a circle and holds hands.

NEW YEAR FACTS

These pages provide more detail about the interesting facts found in the book. They are intended to be used by adults as a learning support to help young readers round out their knowledge of each holiday featured in the *Holidays around the World* series.

Pages 4–5

New Year's Day is celebrated on January 1 every year. In the time of the Romans, the month of March was the beginning of the new year. Julius Caesar introduced a new calendar about 2,000 years ago, changing this to January. However, several countries continued to mark the New Year in December or March. Hundreds of years later, Pope Gregory XIII introduced the Gregorian calendar. This set New Year's Day in January.

Pages 6–7

New Year's Day is celebrated by people all over the world. The world is divided into time zones. The first country to celebrate New Year's Day is an island in the Pacific Ocean called Kiribati. The last is American Samoa.

Pages 8–9

Janus was a Roman god. The ancient Romans believed that Janus was the god of change and beginnings. His two faces were symbolic of looking at both the old and new years. Romans made offerings to Janus on January 1, hoping to bring good luck. They had parties and decorated their homes with greenery, such as laurel branches.

Pages 10–11

Thousands of people go to Times Square in New York City on December 31. People have celebrated New Year's Eve in Times Square since 1907. Today, the countdown and ball drop ceremony are televised all around the world. The ball can be seen year-round at One Times Square. It is made up of 2,688 crystal triangles and more than 32,000 LED lights.

Pages 12–13

Fireworks light up the sky at midnight on January 1. Firework displays are community events where there is often skating, food, and a party beforehand. Major cities of the world hold spectacular displays. Some of the most famous firework displays take place in Sydney, Australia and Paris, France. Fireworks were probably invented in China more than 2,000 years ago.

Pages 14–15

There are special foods to eat on New Year's Day. Different countries have traditional foods that are eaten during this time. In Spain, people eat 12 grapes at midnight on New Year's Day to bring them happiness throughout the coming year. Pomegranates are eaten for good luck in Turkey. Many foods symbolize wealth, good fortune, and prosperity. These include cabbage, black-eyed peas, pork, fish, and noodles.

Pages 16–17

People enjoy going to parades on New Year's Day. The Rose Parade in Pasadena consists of marching bands, horses, and floats decorated with flowers. It began more than 100 years ago as part of a festival to show off the warm weather, flowers, and fruit that abound in California in the middle of winter.

Pages 18–19

Many people make New Year's resolutions. People make resolutions to try to improve their lives. This could involve helping others, such as by volunteering at a food bank or donating money to a charity. They may also try to be kinder and more thoughtful to those around them. The idea originated in ancient Babylon, where people wanted to please the gods at the start of the year.

Pages 20–21

At midnight, people sing "Auld Lang Syne." It was written by a Scottish poet named Robert Burns in 1788. The lyrics are not specifically about the New Year, but describe friends remembering times they spent together in the past. *Auld lang syne* means "since long ago" or "for old times' sake." It became a New Year's tradition in North America when a band, Guy Lombardo and His Royal Canadians, played the song in 1929.

KEY WORDS

Research has shown that as much as 65 percent of all written material published in English is made up of 300 words. These 300 words cannot be taught using pictures or learned by sounding them out. They must be recognized by sight. This book contains 71 common sight words to help young readers improve their reading fluency and comprehension. This book also teaches young readers several important content words, such as proper nouns. These words are paired with pictures to aid in learning and improve understanding.

Page	Sight Words First Appearance
4	a, day, different, every, first, is, it, new, of, on, some, the, year
6	as, been, has
7	about, all, begin, by, over, people, that, time, to, world
8	after, at, back, faces, had, head, him, his, old, one, other, two, was
11	city, down, from, go, in, large, more, than, watch
12	and, family, light, their, up, with
15	are, eat, foods, good, many, states, there, these, thought
16	also
19	help, like, make, might, or, they
20	hands

Page	Content Words First Appearance
4	cultures, date, January, New Year's Day
8	Janus, month, Roman god
11	ball, building, December, midnight, New York City, television, Times Square, top
12	fireworks, friends, sky
15	black-eyed peas, cabbage, ham, luck, United States
16	California, football, game, parades, Pasadena, Rose Parade
19	charity, community, money, promises, resolutions
20	"Auld Lang Syne," circle

Published by Smartbook Media Inc.
350 5th Avenue, 59th Floor New York, NY 10118
Website: www.openlightbox.com

Copyright ©2021 Smartbook Media Inc.
All rights reserved. No part of this publication may be reproduced, stored in a retrieval system, or transmitted in any form or by any means, electronic, mechanical, photocopying, recording, or otherwise, without the prior written permission of the publisher.

Library of Congress Cataloging-in-Publication Data

Names: Daly, Ruth, 1962- author.
Title: New Year / Ruth Daly.
Description: New York : Smarktbook Media Inc., 2020. | Series: Holidays around the world | Audience: Ages 5-7 | Audience: Grades K-1 |
Identifiers: LCCN 2020004825 (print) | LCCN 2020004826 (ebook) | ISBN 9781510553286 (library binding) | ISBN 9781510553293 | ISBN 9781510553309
Subjects: LCSH: New Year--Juvenile literature.
Classification: LCC GT4905 .D355 2020 (print) | LCC GT4905 (ebook) | DDC

394.2614--dc23
LC record available at https://lccn.loc.gov/2020004825
LC ebook record available at https://lccn.loc.gov/2020004826

032020
110819

Printed in Guangzhou, China
1 2 3 4 5 6 7 8 9 0   24 23 22 21 20

Project Coordinator: Priyanka Das
Art Director: Terry Paulhus

Every reasonable effort has been made to trace ownership and to obtain permission to reprint copyright material. The publisher would be pleased to have any errors or omissions brought to its attention so that they may be corrected in subsequent printings.

The publisher acknowledges Alamy, Getty Images, iStock, and Shutterstock as its primary image suppliers for this title.